D0787999

HENRY COLE

Building

KT KATHERINE TEGEN BOOKS
An Imprint of HarperCollins Publishers

Two beavers are searching for
a place to make their home.
It is late winter and still cold.
The trees are still bare.

They find a good spot near a small stream.
There are willow and maple trees nearby.

The two beavers begin to build.
They have strong teeth and jaws.
By chewing and gnawing,
they cut trees down.

They work hard,
chewing and gnawing.
The trees are cut into
smaller pieces.

The beavers haul the cut branches
into the stream
and stick them in the mud.
The freshly cut branches
are sturdy and strong.

Building, building.
That is what beavers do best.

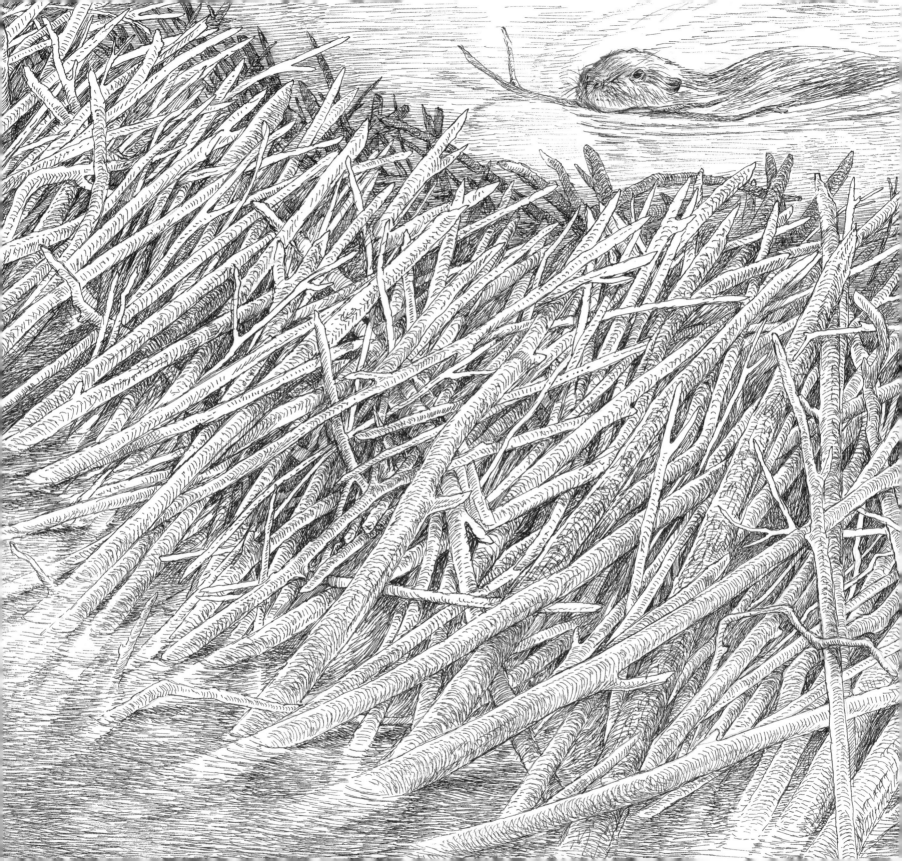

Soon, a small dam is built across the stream.

The dam holds the water back, and a pond forms.

As the beavers make the dam bigger,
the pond grows larger too.

Building, building.
That is what beavers do best.

In the middle of the pond,
they build a dome-shaped lodge.
An underwater passageway leads inside.

It is safe and dark.
The mother beaver can have
her babies inside the lodge.

The babies are born with soft fur.
The mother beaver nurses them,
and they grow stronger.

In a few days, the baby beavers are ready to explore.

Their soft fur keeps them warm in the cold water.

While they explore, a coyote spots them!

Their parents slap their tales on the water.
The loud noise is a signal!
The young beavers dive into the water
and to the safety of the lodge.

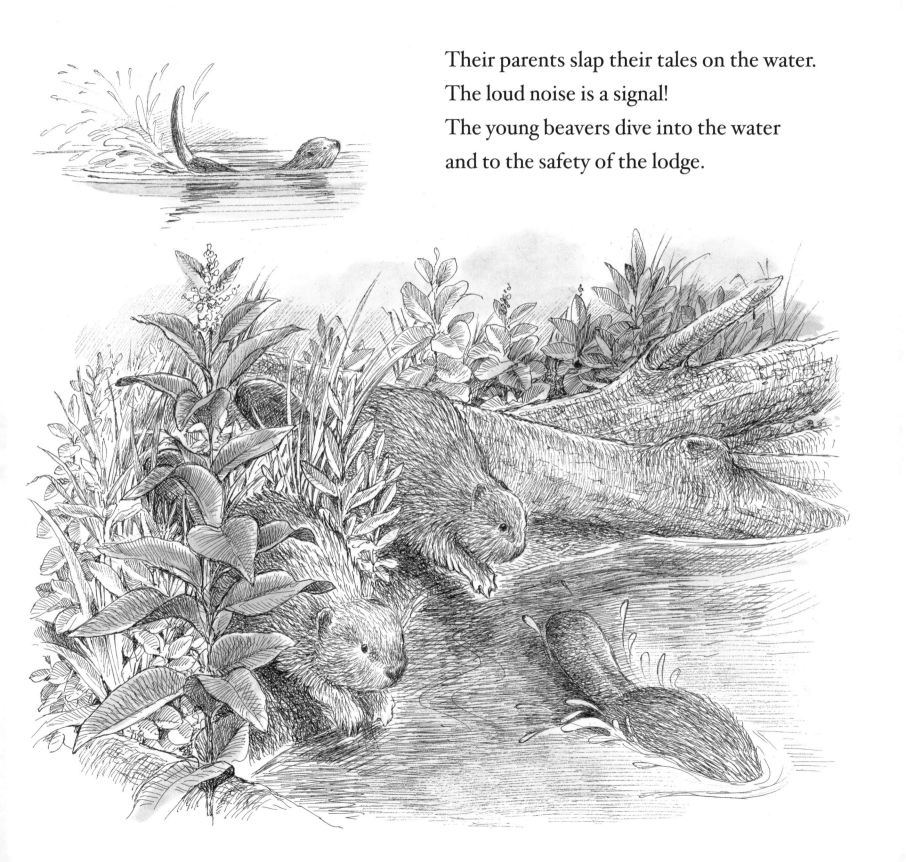

Days pass and the beaver babies grow bigger.
They begin to eat the soft parts of twigs and bark.
The parents watch the babies carefully while
building more of their dam.

Building, building.
That is what beavers do best.

Late one afternoon, a thunderstorm
darkens the sky to the west.
Rain pours from the sky.
It floods the pond and threatens to break the dam.
But the beaver family works hard.
They rebuild what the storm has swept away.

The pond is large now.
Other animals make the pond their home.
There are ducks and blackbirds, butterflies
and swallows, dragonflies and turtles.

The days get shorter.
The willows and maples
lose their leaves.
The beaver family gathers enough twigs
and branches to eat through the winter.

Winter covers the lodge with snow and ice.

The beaver family is warm and protected
while they wait for spring.

AUTHOR'S NOTE

Can you think of an animal that can alter its habitat to suit its needs? You probably thought of humans, but what about the beaver? Beavers are outstanding and important engineers. They can cut trees, build dams, construct lodges, and create wetland environments not only for themselves but for uncounted other plant and animal species. These ponds and flooded areas provide food and shelter for many fish, amphibian, reptile, bird, and aquatic insect species.

Sticks and mud are used for building the dam, blocking a stream or creek. As a pond builds behind the dam, the beavers now have a protected place to live. Their lodge, usually in the middle of the pond, is where they raise two to four young. And the lodge is a cozy place to spend the cold winter.

Beavers need to be on the lookout for predators. Adult beavers will slap their broad tails on the surface of the pond to make a warning sound that says "danger nearby." But although they keep a keen eye out for foxes, wolves, hawks, and coyotes, humans are by far the biggest predator for beavers. A beaver's pelt is very dense with soft fur, and they were hunted nearly to extinction for those valuable pelts. Thanks to protective laws, beavers are becoming more numerous, and can continue creating their wonderful aquatic ecosystems.

Katherine Tegen Books is an imprint of HarperCollins Publishers

Building
Copyright © 2022 by Henry Cole
All rights reserved. Manufactured in Italy.
ISBN 978-0-06-313655-7

The artist used Micropens and acrylic paints to create the illustrations for this book.
Typography by Dana Fritts. Hand lettering by Leah Palmer Preiss
22 23 24 25 26 RTLO 10 9 8 7 6 5 4 3 2 1

First Edition